AF484729

GIVING
God's Way

The Golden Key to the Storehouse of Blessing

ISBN: 979-8-9917801-9-3

Dr. Tom Sexton

GIVING
God's Way

TABLE OF CONTENTS

STEWARDSHIP

The Bible says in I Corinthians 4:1-2, "Let a man so account of us, as of the ministers of Christ, and stewards of the mysteries of God. Moreover it is required in stewards, that a man be found faithful."

> "Moreover it is required in stewards,
>
> that a man be found faithful."

As Bible-believing people, we believe God's Word is the final authority in life.

I Corinthians 6:19 says, "What? know ye not that your body is the temple of the Holy Ghost which is in you, which ye have of God, and ye are not your own?"

In verse nineteen the word "What?" is read like a shocking word. "What?" Did you ever hear someone tell you something that shocked you so much that you said, "What? Say that again!" In I Corinthians 6:19, the word "What?" comes out of shock and dismay.

★ ★ ★ ★ ★

"What? know ye not that your body is the temple of the Holy Ghost which is in you, which ye have of God, and ye are not your own? For ye are bought with a price: therefore glorify God in your body, and in your spirit, which are God's" (I Corinthians 6:19-20).

If you are a Christian, the Bible says you are not your own, you are bought with a price. You belong to the Lord Jesus Christ.

Because you belong to Him, He owns you. He owns me. He owns everything that we have. It is all His. We are simply stewards. The Bible says in I Corinthians 4:2, "Moreover it is required in stewards, that a man be found faithful."

Psalm 50:10 says, "For every beast of the field is mine, and the cattle upon a thousand hills." The Lord said the cattle on a thousand hills, literally every cattle, every beast belongs to the Lord. Not only do they belong to the Lord, but also the hills on which the cattle are standing belong to God.

The Bible says in Haggai 2:8, "The silver is mine, and the gold is mine, saith the LORD of hosts." All the silver and all the gold belong to the Lord. It is all His. You may say, "I have a gold mine." No, you are borrowing that gold mine. It belongs to the Lord. God said all the silver and all the gold and all the precious stones belong to Him.

Psalm 24:1 says, "The earth is the LORD's, and the fulness thereof; the world, and they that dwell therein."

★ ★ ★ ★ ★

Not only does God say that He owns the cattle on a thousand hills and the hills on which the cattle stand. Not only does God say that He owns the silver and gold and all the precious stones.

But God also says the earth is the Lord's, and the fullness thereof, and the world, and they that dwell therein! In other words, God owns everybody and everything.

We have been redeemed and bought with a price. If you do not understand this, then I am going to tell you at the end of this message how to know for sure you are going to heaven. That is the most important thing in the world. God loves you, and Jesus died for you. The Bible says in I Corinthians 6:20, "…Ye are bought with a price…" The price was His precious blood. He shed His blood for you and for me.

I once read the statement that God owns the very air we breathe. Daniel 5:23 says, "…The God in whose hand thy breath is…" When you exhale, remember that it is God who gives you the next breath. God owns everything.

I want you to think about being a good steward. We ought to be good stewards in these three areas: tithing, giving, and faith promise giving.

★ ★ ★ ★ ★

TITHING

We ought to be good stewards in our tithing.

I want to make sure we understand what the Bible has to say about stewardship. You have a choice just like I do. You can choose what the Bible says, or you can choose what you want to believe. I have decided that I am going to believe the Bible.

When I got saved, I made a decision to trust what the Bible says. The preacher told me that God loved me and that Jesus died for me. He said that I owed a debt, and that, because Jesus paid it in full, I could be saved. That night I did what the Bible says to do.

Guess what? It works! Hallelujah! I can tell you it does!

Many times, in my life, I have had to make decisions based solely on what the Bible teaches. When the Bible contradicted what I thought and what I believed, I did what the Bible said to do.

Before I came to know the Lord, a friend asked me, "What do you think about the Bible?" I said, "I believe some of it is true." I did not know the Gospel of John from the book of Genesis. I did not know the difference. He said, "Some of it probably is true."

★ ★ ★ ★ ★

I said, "You know what we could do? We could go through the Bible, find what we think is true, and start a church on what we believe is true."

I am just glad God did not kill me that instant. God could have just said, "That's it. He does not even deserve to live. Zap!" And God would have been merciful! But God was good to let me find out that <u>all</u> the Word of God is true.

We ought to be good stewards in tithing.

God says, "Will a man rob God? Yet ye have robbed me. But ye say, Wherein have we robbed thee? In tithes and offerings. "Ye are cursed with a curse: for ye have robbed me, even this whole nation.

Bring ye all the tithes into the storehouse, that there may be meat in mine house, and prove me now herewith, saith the LORD of hosts, if I will not open you the windows of heaven, and pour you out a blessing, that there shall not be room enough to receive it.

And I will rebuke the devourer for your sakes, and he shall not destroy the fruits of your ground; neither shall your vine cast her fruit before the time in the field, saith the LORD of hosts.

And all nations shall call you blessed: for ye shall be a delightsome land, saith the LORD of hosts." Malachi 3:8-12.

★ ★ ★ ★ ★

God does not own ten percent; God owns everything.

When we talk about tithing, we are talking about what God wants us to do as good stewards

WE ARE TO BRING THE TITHE INTO THE STOREHOUSE

We are to <u>bring</u> the tithe <u>into</u> the storehouse. God's Word says in Malachi 3:10, "<u>Bring</u> ye all the tithes <u>into</u> the store-house…"

The church is the **store**house. The Bible says in I Corinthians 16:2, "Upon the first day of the week let every one of you lay by him in **store**, as God hath prospered him…"

Sunday is "the first day of the week." The world has convinced people that Monday is the first day of the week, but the Bible teaches that Sunday is the first day of the week.

Do you remember when the Lord Jesus was criticized for working miracles on the sabbath, which is Saturday? They wanted to stone Him for doing that. And the Lord Jesus said, "I am Lord of the sabbath."

In other words, He said, "I do not have to go by the sabbath; I made the sabbath for man. The sabbath is man's day. I am Lord over the sabbath. I am Lord over man."

He healed the leper on Saturday, and they said, "Let's kill Him. He violated the sabbath." The Lord Jesus taught that

★ ★ ★ ★ ★

there is a whole lot more to God than just the sabbath. The sabbath was something God did for man.

The Lord Jesus said, "For the Son of man is Lord even of the sabbath day" (Matthew 12:8). They said, "What does He mean by that?" He explained very clearly what He meant on that resurrection morning.

The Bible says on the first day of the week, which is Sunday, they went to the tomb, and the angel said, "He is not here: for he is risen, as he said…" Matthew 28:6.

The Lord Jesus rose from the grave on the first day of the week, which is Sunday, proving that He was Lord over the sabbath and Lord of the sabbath.

He was also demonstrating that Sunday is the Lord's Day. This is why we have church on Sunday, not on Saturday.

Jesus never said that we should keep the sabbath. Of all the commandments that He repeated, He did not repeat Exodus 20:8 which says, "Remember the sabbath day, to keep it holy." He understood that the church would worship on Sunday, the first day of the week.

Therefore, the Bible says in I Corinthians 16:2, "Upon the **first day of the week** let every one of you lay by him in **store**, as God hath prospered him…" Sunday is the day we should tithe to the church which is God's storehouse.

★ ★ ★ ★ ★

THE TITHE IS 10%

The tithe is ten percent. The Bible says in Leviticus 27:32, "…the **tenth** shall be holy unto the LORD." It is holy because it belongs to the Lord.

The Bible says, "You are a holy people." "For thou art an holy people unto the LORD thy God…" (Deuteronomy 7:6, 14:2, 21). You may say, "I don't feel like I am holy. I don't act like I am holy." That is why the Bible says in I Peter 1:16, "…Be ye holy; for I am holy." God says that we should be holy and maintain a testimony for the Lord.

We have in our hands the Holy Bible. As a matter of fact, mine says "The Holy Bible" on the cover. I like those that say "The Holy Bible." It truly is a Holy Bible.

Ten percent belongs to the Lord. In Leviticus 27:32 God's Word says, "The tenth shall be holy unto the LORD."

GOD DOES THREE THINGS FOR US WHEN WE TITHE

1. God prospers us by opening the windows of heaven.

2. God promises to rebuke the devourer.

3. God protects the fruit of our lives.

If we will tithe, God says in Malachi 3:8-11, "I will…open you the windows of heaven, and pour you out a blessing."

★ ★ ★ ★ ★

God promises to prosper us by opening the windows of heaven.

We sing a little song, "The windows of heaven are open. The blessings are falling tonight…" Do you know why we sing that song? Because when we tithe, God opens the windows and pours out a blessing on our lives.

I do not know all the blessings that God has in store for us in our lifetime, but God has a wonderful storehouse filled with the goodness and blessings of God. The Bible says in I Corinthians 2:9 that it has not even entered our minds and hearts what God has prepared for us. "But as it is written, Eye hath not seen, nor ear heard, neither have entered into the heart of man, the things which God hath prepared for them that love him."

How do we get the blessings of God on our lives? Simply by <u>bringing</u> the tithe <u>into</u> the storehouse.

Let me tell you about the old preacher that I heard preach right after I was saved. He preached on **"Giving While You're Living So You're Knowing Where It's Going."**

He was one of those old-fashioned, get-after-it-for-God preachers. He started preaching, and he was tearing it up! He must have been preaching in a dead church because there were not very many hearty "Amens."

He made a statement in that sermon that I have never forgotten. He said, "Here is a great truth that you need to get a hold of. The hole that you give through is the same hole that God blesses you through." (God calls that "hole" a window.)

So, this old preacher said, "**The hole that you give through is the same hole that God blesses you through. Make it BIG!**" I thought, "Praise God for that! That is the way it ought to be."

I believe there are some Christians who have the window of heaven just barely cracked open, and the blessings have to be slipped through and thrown out like pieces of paper floating down.

Then there are those who have a hole in the window the size of a straw, and the blessings have to be wadded up like little spit-balls and spit down to them.

Then there are some who just open the window all the way, and God backs up the holy dump trucks and pours out the blessings on their lives. I want to be the kind of Christian who has the window wide open. "The windows of heaven are open. The blessings are falling tonight."

That is a promise from God. The same God who said in John 10:28, "I give unto them eternal life; and they shall never perish." He is the same God who said He's building a mansion in Heaven for you, and is the same God who said in Malachi 3:10, "I will…open you the windows of heaven, and pour you out a blessing." We should tithe because God blesses us when we do.

★ ★ ★ ★ ★

Not only should we tithe because God promises to prosper us, but we should also bring the tithe because **God promises to rebuke the devourer**. He says in Malachi 3:11, "I will rebuke the devourer for your sakes…"

The Devil is real. He is alive. He does not run around in a little red outfit with his tail hanging out and a pitchfork in his hand. That is not what he looks like. As a matter of fact, the Bible says he can transform himself into an angel of light. He can appear to be an angel of light.

God says if you will bring the tithe into the storehouse, He will rebuke the devourer. The devourer is the one who wants to destroy God's people.

I Peter 5:8 says, "Be sober, be vigilant; because your adversary the devil, as a roaring lion, walketh about, seeking whom he may **devour**."

Devour means "to make disappear." There are many people who disappear. I do not mean they disappear off the face of the earth, I mean they disappear out of churches. They are no longer teaching Sunday school, working on a bus route, or singing in the choir. They have disappeared. Many people disappear out of homes. There are many marriages from which one of the mates have disappeared, the husband or the wife. There are many children that disappear.

You ask, "What causes that?" The Bible says the Devil is a devourer of God's people; he causes them to disappear.

★ ★ ★ ★ ★

God's Word says if you will bring the tithe into the storehouse, He will rebuke the devourer. The Devil will not devour you. I would bring the tithe into the storehouse if for no other reason than to get God to rebuke the Devil.

I have heard people say, "I rebuke the Devil." I do not know about that, but I will tell you one thing, when God speaks the Devil must listen. And God says, "When you bring the tithe into the storehouse, I will not only open the windows of heaven, but also I will rebuke the devourer." The Devil has to listen to God.

The Devil has to listen to the Lord Jesus because He has the keys to death and hell, and He will lock the Devil up one day. In Matthew 8:29, the maniac had demons, and they said, "Art thou come hither to torment us before the time?" They knew that all the Lord Jesus had to do was speak, and they would be chained and bound forever.

All He had to do was speak the word, and every demon in hell would be bound forever. The same God said, "I will rebuke the devourer."

Many Christians have the Devil hot on their trail. Many Christians are fighting everything you can imagine. They have trouble in the family. They have trouble with their children. They have trouble with a rebellious child. They wonder what in the world is going on. They need to take care of what God commands them to do, and He will help them with their children.

★ ★ ★ ★ ★

If I had a problem with one of my children, and they were being devoured, I would make sure I was tithing. Get that right first. We need to make sure we are not robbing God.

God also promises that when we tithe, **He will protect our fruit**. We have a lot of fruit. The most precious fruit we have is our families. I want God to protect my fruit.

I have the power, and so do you, as a Christian, to assure the windows of heaven are open for the blessings of God on my life. I have the power, as a Christian, to have God intervene on my behalf and rebuke the devourer. I have the power, as a Christian, to have God protect my fruit.

This is all done when I do what God says and <u>bring</u> the tithe into the <u>storehouse</u>.

Here are some questions people often ask:

Is tithing a practice for this age?

The answer is simple. Tithing is taught and practiced all through the Bible and is not limited to one age.

People ask, "Preacher, is tithing for this age? Isn't that an Old Testament saying?" In the Old Testament, God says, "Thou shalt not kill." Are you glad we still practice that? We like pulling Old Testament things out that we like, but we do not like some of them. Let me answer that question, "Is tithing for this age?"

First of all, **tithing was practiced before the Law,** before God gave the Law. Tithing was practiced in Genesis 14:20 when Abraham gave a tithe to Melchizedek. Melchizedek is a type of Christ. The Bible says, "And he gave him tithes of all."

Tithing was taught and practiced under the Law. Of course, we understand that. Leviticus 27:30 says, "And all the tithe…is the LORD's: it is holy unto the LORD."

Tithing was confirmed by the Lord Jesus. If for no other reason, you should tithe because the Lord Jesus said in Matthew 23:23, "…Ye pay tithe of mint and anise and cummin, …these ought ye to have done…"

> ### Should I tithe if I cannot afford to?
>
> We should not ask ourselves if we can afford to tithe.
>
> We should ask ourselves if we want to live the life of a thief.

★ ★ ★ ★ ★

The second question people often ask is this: "Should I tithe if I cannot afford to?" That is a good question.

We have to realize something. One hundred percent belongs to God. It is not ten percent God's and ninety percent ours. Everything we have belongs to God. As stewards, we have to decide whether we are going to honor God with what is His.

I like to look at it like this. Tithing is not bringing a tenth to the Lord. Tithing is when I get paid. I bring God the tenth, and He gives me ninety percent. That is why it is said that **the tithe ought to be the first check written**. Proverbs 3:9 says, "Honour the LORD with thy substance, and with the **first**fruits of all thine increase."

Think about this. Most people wait until the end and say, "Well, let's see now. I have the car payment and the boat payment and my little fund and my retirement plan going, and I don't have but a couple of dollars left. I don't think I can pay God this week." They have it all turned around.

You see, the Devil is a master at reversing things. Did you know that? I learned a great truth when I was a new Christian. The Devil is the complete opposite of God.

God saves your soul, you give Him your body, and He renews your mind. That is what the Bible says in Romans 12:1 and 2. The Devil is the complete opposite. He wants your mind, to get your body, to condemn your soul.

★ ★ ★ ★ ★

God says the man is the head of the house, the wife is to submit and follow, and the children are to obey. The Devil says the complete opposite. In the Devil's house, the children are in charge, the mother submits to them, and then they all turn on the dad and convince him he needs to do what is "best" for their family.

That is not God's way. That is the Devil's way.

Do not let the Devil reverse it on you. **Tithing is not paying God ten percent. Tithing is when God gives you ninety percent.** In other words, it all belongs to God, but ninety percent is not yours until first you give God what He wants.

I Corinthians 3:9 says, "For we are labourers together with God…" God is our partner. Can you imagine that God is in partnership with us? He owns everything. He owns the cattle on a thousand hills. He owns the gold and the silver. He owns everybody. Yet God says, "I will form a partnership with you, and I will be good to you. I will pay you ninety percent, and I will keep only ten percent."

God says, "I am going to keep ten percent." But we say, "Wait a minute. One hundred percent is mine, and I will take what I need first, and then give what is left over to God." That is not right.

God says it this way in Malachi 3:8, "Will a man rob God?" The truth is, **we are not honest with God until we first give God the ten percent that belongs to Him.**

     ★ ★ ★ ★ ★

You may say, "I am not sure I can figure out ten percent." Then make it twenty percent to be safe. Go ahead and tithe thirty percent and make the Devil really angry! You cannot out-give God.

I met a man once who said, "Preacher, one day I decided I was going to tithe by faith, too."

I said, "I have never heard of faith-tithing."

He said, "I know what I make, but I am going to start tithing on what I want to make. By faith I am going to start." So, he started tithing on what he wanted to make.

He said, "Do you know what I found out? God made sure that He was not in debt to me. The more I tithed the more God increased my income." He said, "I have a little game going with God. I try to figure out how I can beat God at this, and God keeps winning." God does not want to be in debt to anyone.

God does not want anyone robbing Him, and God says to bring the tithe. **The tithe is the first ten percent, not the last ten percent.** When we give God the ten percent that belongs to Him, God gives us the ninety percent that is left. What a Saviour we have that will do something like that!

Can you imagine your boss coming up to you and saying, "Now, listen. We made $10,000.00 this week. Here it is." You say to the boss, "Okay, here is $1,000.00 for you." He says, "All right. Here is $9,000.00 for you."

★ ★ ★ ★ ★

The next week you go in, and he says, "We made $10,000.00 again." You say, "Now this week I need $9,999.00." He says, "I am sorry. Now you get nothing. You give me my ten percent first, and I will give you what is left. If you think you are going to take what you want and give me what is left, we are not doing business anymore." You would be wise to give him what he wants first.

You may say, "I cannot afford to tithe." No, wait a minute, you can't afford not to tithe!

The child of God should not be considering the question of whether or not he can afford to tithe. He should ask himself if he wants to live the life of a thief.

Should I give my tithe to the local church?

Yes. The church is the storehouse. All through the book of Acts, you will find God's people bringing their offering to their local church.

Here is another question people ask. "Should I give my tithe to the local church?"

Yes, the local church is the storehouse. "<u>Bring</u> ye all the tithes <u>into</u> the storehouse…"

★ ★ ★ ★ ★

People say, "I believe in the 'universal' church." They do not know what they are saying. See if that 'universal' pastor will help them!

Acts 1:8 says, "…And ye shall be witnesses unto me both in Jerusalem…" First of all, we must reach Jerusalem. Then we need to reach Judaea and Samaria, and then the uttermost part of the earth. But we must start in our Jerusalem.

How do you reach your Jerusalem? Do you call those TV preachers? Do you send them your tithe? Call them when you have problems! You will find out they will pick up the phone and try to find a local church! A local church is going to help you.

Once a man said to me, "My former pastor told me if I didn't agree with the church, I didn't have to give them my tithe."

I said, "Really? That's interesting. What did he say to do with it?"

"He said I should put it in a coffee can. Then when I find a church that I can agree with, I can give it to them."

I prayed, "Lord, give me something that this man will understand." God gave me this as I was talking to him.

I said, "The Lord Jesus is our example. Do you believe that?"

He said, "Yes, I do."

★ ★ ★ ★ ★

I said, "He is our example. As a matter of fact, He is every Christian's example. If we have any questions about what we should do, we should do what Jesus did. We should follow in His steps, follow His example. I Peter 2:21-22 says, '…Ye should follow his steps: Who did no sin, neither was guile found in his mouth.'

"Let me ask you something. Do you think the Lord Jesus worked? He was known as the carpenter's son. He was a carpenter. Do you think He worked?

He said, "Oh, yes, no doubt about it. He worked."

I said, "When He worked, He got paid. He was a working man. As a working man, He made some money. What do you think He did with that money? Did He tithe?

"Well, He must have tithed because in John 8:46, He asked the Pharisees and scribes and all those religious people who tried to find fault with Him, 'Which of you convinceth Me of sin?' If they could have put their finger on one thing, they could have proven He was not Christ.

He also made this statement that no one else has ever made. He said in Matthew 5:17 that He came to fulfill the Law.

Sitting in that crowd among His critics was one rabbi who knew Him, because he was the rabbi in the synagogue that He attended.

If Jesus was a God-robber, if Jesus did not tithe, that rabbi

★ ★ ★ ★ ★

would have stood up and said, 'I bring accusation against Him. I have known Him for thirty years. I have never known Him to bring the tithe into the storehouse.'

The fact that no one was able to accuse the Lord Jesus of disobeying God's Word is proof that He was a tither.

Did the Lord Jesus agree with everything that went on in the synagogue? No. The Bible tells of the Lord Jesus overturning the moneychangers' tables and saying they had made His Father's house a den of thieves. Yet He still brought the tithe.

Even if a person disagrees with some practice in their local church, that is not grounds for disobeying the Lord's command."

Tithing is not giving; it is bringing. When we tithe, we are bringing to the Lord what already belongs to Him.

Let me illustrate. Imagine that Tim loans his car to Glenn. No one knows that the car belongs to Tim. Glenn is just going to borrow the car for two days.

After two days, Glenn does not bring the car back to Tim. As a matter of fact, Glenn begins to tell everyone that it is his car. He puts his name on the front plate.

Finally, Tim comes to me and says, "Pastor, I do not have a car." He does not tell me what happened to his. Glenn has been driving his car for three months now.

★ ★ ★ ★ ★

I come to church and say, "I would like everyone to help us today with an offering for Brother Tim's car. Brother Tim needs an automobile. He is having to walk. You can have a part."

People begin to give towards Tim's car fund. Everybody has a part in Tim's car. Some people give one hundred dollars, some give two hundred dollars, and others are able to give more.

Then Glenn comes forward and says, "God has been good to me. I am going to give him my car." And he throws the keys in the basket. "Praise God! I gave him my car."

We all say, "Isn't Glenn some kind of giver!" We do not know that this car is the same car that belonged to Tim before Glenn took it over. Do you understand what I am illustrating?

People say, "I am giving my tithe." No, it is not your tithe to start with. How in the world can you give it? It is God's tithe. You do not give someone something that is theirs; you bring it back to them. The tithe belongs to God. You do not give it. I do not give it. We bring it. When we do not bring it, we are robbing God. "Bring ye all the tithes…"

By the way, do not ask anybody to try to figure this out. Do not sit down with pencil and paper and figure out if you can afford to tithe. You will come up every time with the answer, No.

★ ★ ★ ★ ★

When I got saved, I owed a whole lot more than my income, especially after I started earning a living the honest way. My income was drastically cut after I got saved. I thought, "What in the world am I going to do? Maybe I can just work hard and get my debts paid and then I can tithe."

I asked my preacher, "What should I do?"

Brother Riley said, "Do not rob God. You tithe."

So, I said, "Okay." By faith my wife and I brought the tithe into the storehouse.

When I went to Bible college, we had a tremendous amount of expense on our home, and I did not make enough money to pay all of the bills, but by faith we tithed.

There were Mondays that we started off with nothing but pocket change, and sometimes we did not even have pocket change, but I am here to say that God has met every need that we have ever had.

God has opened the windows of heaven and blessed us. God has been good to us. We did not sit down and figure out whether we could tithe. We just went ahead and did what we should. And God took care of us.

You say, "Preacher, I want to be a good steward." Are you a tither? Are you bringing the tithe to the Lord?

★ ★ ★ ★ ★

GIVING

We ought to be good stewards in giving. Giving does not come from the ten percent. Giving should come from the ninety percent that you have left.

You may say, "I do not have much left out of the ninety percent after I pay my bills." Then start working to try to get something. Figure out what you can do sacrificially.

The Bible says in Luke 6:38, "**Give**, and it shall be given unto you; good measure, pressed down, and shaken together, and running over, shall men give into your bosom. For with the same measure that ye mete withal it shall be measured to you again."

The Bible does not say "Bring" in this verse, the Bible says "**Give.**" **You do not give the tithe; you bring the tithe. But the remaining ninety percent is yours, and God says to give out of that.** You give, and God will bless your life.

Giving is not tithing. Tithing is not giving. Let me say that again. Giving is not tithing. Tithing is not giving.

A pastor friend of mine was telling me about his first job. He was a teenager and made twenty dollars. His Christian mother sat down with him and asked, "What belongs to God?" Jim said he took two dollars and put it aside.

Then she asked, "What are you going to give the Lord?" He said, "Here is my offering, this two dollars." She said, "That

★ ★ ★ ★ ★

is not yours, that is the Lord's. Your offering comes out of the eighteen dollars you have left after the tithe."

Brother Odom told me that was one of the greatest lessons he has ever learned about giving.

Many people believe they have given when they tithe. However, our giving comes out of the ninety percent that is left after the tithe.

Tithing is bringing the ten percent. Giving comes out of the ninety percent.

When you give, God says He will give to you. When you give, God says men shall give into your bosom.

Many faithful Christians have had promotions and wonder, "How in the world did I get a promotion?" I will tell you how. They did what God wanted them to do. They gave, and God made sure men gave to them.

Some Christians cannot explain the things that have happened. They bought a piece of property that later became very valuable. How in the world did that happen? Are they such geniuses? No, they gave, and God made sure men gave to them. That is the way it works.

If you will read the book of Acts, you will find out that God's people gave. They gave sacrificially. God not only wants us to tithe, but God also wants us to give.

★ ★ ★ ★ ★

You cannot explain it any other way. God will bless you if you give. Whatever you do will prosper. God will make sure that people will come and give into your bosom. He will make sure that you have your needs met. If you will give, God will take care of you.

FAITH-PROMISE GIVING

The Bible says in II Corinthians 8:1-5, "Moreover, brethren, we do you to wit of the grace of God bestowed on the churches of Macedonia;

How that in a great trial of affliction the abundance of their joy and their deep poverty abounded unto the riches of their liberality.

For to their power, I bear record, yea, and **beyond their power they were willing** of themselves;

Praying us with much intreaty that we would receive the gift, and take upon us the fellowship of the ministering to the saints.

And this they did, not as we hoped, but first gave their own selves to the Lord, and unto us by the will of God."

"…Beyond their power they were willing…"

★ ★ ★ ★ ★

Faith-promise giving is asking the Lord to let us give beyond ourselves. Faith-promise giving is for Christians who have become faithful tithers and have given sacrificially out of their budget for the cause of Christ, yet want to do more, beyond their power.

Faith-promise giving is asking God to lay upon our hearts an amount that He will give to us. Faith-promise giving is asking God for something, and God answers you and blesses your life. It can begin so small.

I remember when we lived in Chattanooga, and we had a 1974 Matador, an ugly car. The vinyl top was peeling off of it.

Inside we had to pin up the top if we wanted to talk to each other. We had to hold up the headliner and say, "Hey, calm down back there, girls!" It was like riding around in a tent that fell in on us. How many of you know what I am talking about? It was so ugly.

I would take the girls to school, and Mandy would say, "Daddy, let us out around the corner, please. Please, Dad, don't pull up in front." We would get out of the car and have to dust the lint off of ourselves, that fell from the ceiling, from every time we hit a bump.

I am talking about one ugly car. That was our family car. That was our only car. Things were very tight.

I was driving to downtown Chattanooga, one day, to go to the courthouse. They were notorious for writing parking

★ ★ ★ ★ ★

tickets at the courthouse. I was going down the road and realized I did not have any money, none at all.

I said to the Lord, "I have to go to the courthouse, and I cannot afford a ticket. Lord, I need a parking space with some time on it, and I am in a hurry. Could You give me one close so I can get in and get out really quickly?"

I was almost ready to turn around, before I ever got to the courthouse, to go back and ask somebody for a quarter, or to pull over and start looking in the seats for quarters.

But I came to a red light right in front of the courthouse. To my surprise, right across the street was a man walking to his car. He got in while the light was still red, started his car up, put it in reverse, and very quickly backed out.

When the light turned green, he pulled out, and I pulled into his spot with thirty minutes left on the meter, right at the front door of the courthouse!

I got out of that car and said, "Whoo! God is good!" I was walking ten feet high off the ground. I said, "God is so good to me!"

People were looking at me and looking at that car and thinking, "What is he talking about?"

I said, "God is so good. What a Saviour! He gave me a twenty-five-cent parking space right at the front door!"

★ ★ ★ ★ ★

About that time God touched my heart. It might have been God, or it might have been the Devil. He said, "You fool, you should have asked for a new car." One time in my miserable life I was on praying ground and I wasted it on a little twenty-five-cent parking meter. I could have said, "Lord, I hate this old car."

God would have just handed me the keys to a Cadillac.

I have never been able to get back on that level of spirituality since then. There is so much I could have done! I had ahold of heaven! I could have had God's power and blessing, instead I got a twenty-five-cent parking place.

But seriously, I cannot tell you how much that has meant to me over the years.

When I told my wife we were going to Cape Coral, to start the Gulf Coast Baptist Church, she asked, "How are we going to live?" I said, "We are going to trust God." She said, "Okay."

We came to Cape Coral and started knocking on doors. We had just enough money to live for just a few weeks. We did not even have enough money to rent the building past the month of deposit we gave them. We did not have the money for anything.

We just believed God could do what He said He would do.

★ ★ ★ ★ ★

Every time I begin to wonder, "Can God? Can God do something? Can He do it?" God reminds me of that twenty-five-cent parking meter. If God is concerned enough about us to give us time on a parking meter, I want you to know God is concerned enough to take care of every need we have.

Can you imagine what it would mean to young people if they prayed for something specifically like that, and God gave it to them?

That twenty-five-cent parking space prayer was many years ago, but God still stirs up my heart about it and still strengthens my faith because of it! There have been many, many times since then when God has proven Himself. But in that one thing, God really showed something to me, and I realized that **faith giving is not how God raises money, but how God matures His children.**

Many Christians never get to that level. They never say, "Let's pray for ten dollars. Let's pray for this. Let's pray for that."

They never get serious about it and say, "Lord, we do not have any more money. We brought the tithe. We sacrificed as much as we could sacrifice. But oh God, there is a need here, and we believe You want to meet that need. If You would let us, by faith, have a part in it, help us, dear Lord. Meet us in the need. Lord God, prove that we are Your children. Give us something so we can make a difference in the lives of people. Oh God, You own the cattle on a thousand hills. You own the gold. You own the land. You own the earth.

★ ★ ★ ★ ★

Oh God, help us meet this need."

God wants us to live beyond our power. God does not call us to do what we can do in our own power. God does not call us to do what we can do with our own abilities and talents. God does not call us to do the possible.

God calls us to do the impossible!

Oh, let us not see what we can do. Let us see what God can do. God's Word says in Luke 1:37, "For with God nothing shall be impossible."

Let me ask you a question. Do you want to be a good steward? The Bible says in I Corinthians 4:2, "Moreover it is required in stewards, that a man be found faithful."

What Kind of Stewards Are We?

The Bible says, "For we must all appear before the judgment seat of Christ; that every one may receive the things done in his body, according to that he hath done, whether it be good or bad." II Corinthians 5:10.

There are two people the Lord Jesus used during His earthly ministry to help us understand the difference between giving and keeping. We see both types in our day.

First, there is Mary, the woman who broke her alabaster box and poured it all on Jesus, Her life is a challenge to follow.

★ ★ ★ ★ ★

Breaking Your Alabaster Box

Second, there is the unnamed man who pulled down his barns so he could keep everything. His life is a warning to all who think about keeping all the blessings of God for self.

Pulling Down Our Barns

As you read the next two chapters determine which one you want to be known as.

★ ★ ★ ★ ★

BREAKING YOUR ALABASTER BOX

"And being in Bethany in the house of Simon the leper, as He sat at meat, there came a woman having an alabaster box of ointment of spikenard very precious; and she brake the box, and poured it on His head.

And there were some that had indignation within themselves, and said, Why was this waste of the ointment made?

For it might have been sold for more than three hundred pence, and have been given to the poor. And they murmured against her.

And Jesus said, Let her alone; why trouble ye her? she hath wrought a good work on Me. For ye have the poor with you always, and whensoever ye will ye may do them good: but Me ye have not always.

She hath done what she could: she is come aforehand to anoint My body to the burying.

Verily I say unto you, Wheresoever this gospel shall be preached throughout the whole world, this also that she hath done shall be spoken of for a memorial of her." Mark 14:3-9.

★ ★ ★ ★ ★

This event took place during the last week of our LORD's earthly ministry. In a few days He would be crucified, so He was trying to prepare His disciples for what was ahead. He spoke to them on various occasions about this.

The first time He mentioned going to Calvary to die, Simon Peter rebuked Him; and for that, the LORD Jesus said to him, "Get thee behind Me, Satan" Mark 8:33.

Ever since I first read that statement, I've been suspicious about those who say to me, "I'm behind you, Preacher." That's where the devil is, and I don't want people back there with him on his team. I want people to get out here beside me where we'll both be shot!

On that first occasion, He was not able to teach them great truth.

Then on another occasion He talked about Calvary, and James and John via their mother asked for the best seats in the kingdom.

"Grant that these my two sons may sit, the one on Thy right hand, and the other on the left, in Thy kingdom.

But Jesus answered and said, Ye know not what ye ask." Matthew 20:21, 22.

But now Jesus is at Simon the leper's house in Bethany. This was an unusual place for Him to be. Simon is cleansed and home with his family, and he is holding a feast. Sitting at the

★ ★ ★ ★ ★

table with the LORD Jesus is not just Simon the leper but "Lazarus…which had been dead, whom He raised from the dead" John 12:1.

Wouldn't that have been something to see? Both the cleansed leper and the resurrected Lazarus were sitting with Jesus and enjoying fellowship with each other.

Then, entering from another room, comes a woman named Mary. She has an alabaster box full of ointment in her hands, "and she brake the box, and poured it on His head" Mark 14:3.

Then "Mary…anointed the feet of Jesus, and wiped His feet with her hair: and the house was filled with the odour of the ointment" (John 12:3). What a night! Mary did something that God mightily used, and I want you to think about breaking your own alabaster box.

Nothing ever gets done for God without somebody breaking their alabaster box and taking care of what needs to be done.

The Bible says that the LORD Jesus was going down to Galilee to minister to the people there and do a great work.

"He went throughout every city and village, preaching and shewing the glad tidings of the kingdom of God: and the twelve were with Him, And certain women, which had been healed of evil spirits and infirmities, Mary called Magdalene, out of whom went seven devils,

★ ★ ★ ★ ★

And Joanna the wife of Chuza Herod's steward, and Susanna, and many others, which ministered unto Him of their substance." Luke 8:1-3.

These women who "ministered unto Him of their substance" made it possible for the LORD Jesus to do something in Galilee. God is always looking for those who will break their alabaster box and do great and mighty things for God with their lives.

MARY'S REASON FOR DOING IT

Why did Mary break the alabaster box? The ointment, inside the alabaster box, was worth at that time almost a year's salary for a man and possibly three years' salary for a woman. Why would Mary take this expensive ointment and pour it on Jesus?

Because of What Jesus Had Done for Her.

She did it because she loved Jesus and because of what He had done for her. The LORD had allowed a tragedy to come into the lives of Mary; her brother, Lazarus; and her sister, Martha.

Lazarus became so ill that there was nothing that the doctors could do to help him, so Mary and Martha sent for Jesus.

"When He [Jesus] had heard therefore that he was sick, He abode two days still in the same place where He was" John 11:6.

★ ★ ★ ★ ★

Jesus delayed His going to see Lazarus, and finally Lazarus died. That's a hard thing to understand if you are Mary and Martha waiting on the LORD.

Have you ever had the LORD delay His coming in your life? Has something come into your life that was so serious and needful that you couldn't fix it; and when you prayed, nothing happened; it seemed as if Heaven was closed? Have you ever been disappointed with the way the LORD worked in your life?

We've all experienced God's delays, and we question what He is doing. But God had a plan and a purpose in Lazarus' sickness and in his death.

When the LORD Jesus came, He spoke to Martha first. Mary was still inside the house. She knew the LORD Jesus was there, but in her heart something was not right. Martha called her and said, "The Master is come, and calleth for thee" v 28.

One of the reasons that the LORD Jesus delayed His coming to Mary and Martha's house was that He was trying to work in Mary's life. I thank God that there was a time when He brought some things into my life that I could not fix myself. I thank God that there was a day in my life when the Master came and 'called for me.'

I am glad that there was a day when I saw the need of Jesus Christ in my life; when I realized that I was a lost sinner on my way to a devil's hell; when I heard the good news of the

★ ★ ★ ★ ★

Gospel and I turned my life over to Christ and trusted Him as my personal Savior. I thank God that I am now saved and on my way to Heaven.

If you have ever had God work in your life to get you to the place where you surrendered to Him, then you can understand why the LORD worked this way in Mary's life.

Mary loved Jesus for what He had done in her life. Aren't you glad that He still works in our lives? Aren't you glad that He stops us and gets our attention? If He didn't work in circumstances in our lives, sometimes we would be far away from what He wanted us to do. He is as much in disturbances and circumstances as He is in deliverances.

One of my favorite verses is Psalm 143:8: "Cause me to hear Thy lovingkindness in the morning; for in Thee do I trust: cause me to know the way wherein I should walk; for I lift up my soul unto Thee."

Dear Friend, there are times when the LORD brings things into our lives to get our attention, and that's how He was working in Mary's life. He got her attention and then changed the direction of her life. "The Master is come, and calleth for thee."

Maybe you are now going through some things in your life, and you wonder what is happening. Maybe the LORD is trying to get your attention.

★ ★ ★ ★ ★

Because of What Jesus Had Done for Her Family.

Another reason Mary broke her alabaster box was because of what Christ had done for her family. Her brother had gotten so sick that he had died—you can't get any worse than that—and they buried him. When the LORD Jesus came, Mary said, 'If You'd have been here, Lazarus would not have died!'

Jesus reminded her, "I am the resurrection, and the life: he that believeth in Me, though he were dead, yet shall he live" John 11:25.

Then Jesus went to the grave of Lazarus. "He cried with a loud voice, Lazarus, come forth. "And he that was dead came forth, bound hand and foot with graveclothes: and his face was bound about with a napkin. Jesus saith unto them, Loose him, and let him go." John 11:43,44.

I like what the old preacher said, that if the LORD Jesus had not called Lazarus by name, every person who had ever died would have come back to life because of the power of His Word.

What a day that was when God brought Mary's brother back to life!

I thank God for what He has brought into my life. Can you imagine God's saving a teenage boy named Clarence Sexton; then calling him to preach; then saving his brother, Tom Sexton; and their mother and sisters and then their "Pop"?

★ ★ ★ ★ ★

How good God is to do that for the Sexton family! What a Saviour we have!

We ought to love Him enough to break our alabaster box because of what He has done for us and what He has done for our families. Whole families are on their way to Heaven because of what the LORD has done for them! God can save your whole household.

The apostle Paul and Silas gave this testimony to the jailer when he asked, "Sirs, what must I do to be saved?

"And they said, Believe on the Lord Jesus Christ, and thou shalt be saved, and thy house." Acts 16:30, 31.

If your family is not saved, you ought to get serious about getting them saved and claim this promise of God that Paul gave to the jailer. Paul could make that statement with conviction because before he got saved, he had family members who were already saved.

"Salute Andronicus and Junia, my kinsmen, and my fellow-prisoners, who are of note among the apostles, who also were in Christ before me." Romans 16:7. Paul's sister prayed that God might save her brother. At that time, he was called Saul, and he was a tough case. It wasn't easy to get his attention. So, she prayed and asked God to do something, and God reached down on the road to Damascus, got Saul's attention, turned his life around, saved him, and then used him mightily.

★ ★ ★ ★ ★

Later, this same sister's son "heard of their lying in wait [to kill his uncle Paul], he went and entered into the castle, and told Paul" Acts 23:16.

No wonder Paul could say with certainty, "Believe on the Lord Jesus Christ, and thou shalt be saved, and thy house"!

We need to seize the moment of opportunity to see our family and friends come to know the LORD. We ought to become desperate about our unsaved family members and become desperate about asking God to work in their lives.

Our father died when we were young, and my mother was widowed with four children. My father had lived a hard life and suffered greatly in the final days of his life, spending them in a care facility similar to our nursing homes or Hope Hospice.

Several years after my brother Clarence had been preaching, a dear preacher came up to him and said that he used to go to a place on Sunday afternoons and hold services. He told my brother that he had met a man and thought because his last name was Sexton he might have been related to us.

When he told my brother that the man's name was Preston Sexton, my brother said, "That was my father." This dear preacher informed him that our father had trusted Christ as his personal Saviour in the final days of his life and had shown a real interest in the things of God.

★ ★ ★ ★ ★

Thank God for those who give their time to help people in nursing homes to know Christ. Imagine God's saving my father and then my brother hearing about it years after he'd been preaching.

I rejoice when people get saved in our church, and we work hard at soul winning.

We had a teenage girl get saved, and she began praying for her father to get saved. He had left her mother and had been gone for three months, but God got ahold of his heart, and he got saved. God brought him back home to his family. It should thrill our hearts when we see families getting saved.

Because of What Jesus Had Done for Their Friends in Bethany.

"Then many of the Jews which came to Mary, and had seen the things which Jesus did, believed on Him." John 11:45. God got their attention! Before Lazarus' death, can't you picture Mary and Martha and Lazarus telling their neighbors what God had done in their lives, telling them about the LORD Jesus and pleading with them to trust the LORD?

But they rejected what was told to them until one day God brought something into all their lives with which they could not deal, something that only God could fix.

Jesus delayed His coming long enough to get everybody's attention; and then, because His timing was right, the LORD

★ ★ ★ ★ ★

Jesus came and not only brought Lazarus back from the dead, but He also saved their friends in Bethany.

And God is still able to save! "Whosoever shall call upon the name of the Lord shall be saved." Romans 10:13. Mary started thinking about what God had done for her and her family and what He had done in her neighborhood and among her friends, and she could not help but love Jesus.

The Holy Spirit put something in her heart to do: she came and broke this alabaster box full of ointment. She didn't take off the lid and pour out just a little; she broke it and poured every drop over the LORD Jesus.

If you know the Savior; if you know that you are going to Heaven; if you know that you are not going to spend eternity in a devil's hell; if you have had the joy and privilege of seeing your loved ones come to Christ; if you have seen God work in the lives of people you know and love, then, dear Friend, you have a reason to break the alabaster box at the LORD Jesus' feet!

THE CROWD's REACTION

What was the crowd's reaction? It is amazing what they said. In fact, in the three Gospels where this story is told, we get the reactions of three different groups of people.

The "Do Nothing" Crowd.

These are those who thought it should not have been done.

"Then saith one of His disciples, Judas Iscariot, Simon's son, which should betray Him, Why was not this ointment sold for three hundred pence, and given to the poor?

This he said, not that he cared for the poor; but because he was a thief, and had the bag, and bare what was put therein."
John 12:4-6.

We should not be surprised at Judas Iscariot's reaction, nor should we be surprised that there is a Judas crowd around today. In fact, you have to climb over them to do anything.

Every time you get excited about God, every time you start to do something for Him, the Judas crowd won't like it at all. In fact, they don't think anything should ever be done for the LORD Jesus.

They think it is terrible when Christians give up a Wednesday night to go to church in the middle of the week instead of playing ball with the team. They think it is crazy to give money or time to a ministry. This crowd doesn't want anything done.

The "Measure and Pour" Crowd.

These are the ones who thought it should have been measured out, not poured out.

"Now when Jesus was in Bethany, in the house of Simon the leper,

★ ★ ★ ★ ★

There came unto Him a woman having an alabaster box of very precious ointment, and poured it on His head, as He sat at meat.

But when His disciples saw it, they had indignation, saying, To what purpose is this waste?" Matthew 26:6-8.

The disciples didn't mind Mary's pouring ointment on the LORD Jesus, but they thought she got carried away with it. They thought she was a little too crazy about it. Why not use just a little bit? Why waste it all on Him?

That's the crowd that puts in exactly what their tithe is and that's it - not one penny beyond that amount. When you say, "Show up on Sunday morning, Sunday night, Wednesday night, and visitation night," they will ask, "How many hours do you want from us, Preacher?"

This crowd will measure out their lives until the trumpet sounds, and this crowd has never done anything great for God! They will take off the alabaster box lid, but they'll only pour out what is absolutely necessary.

They don't understand what Mary saw or what she got ahold of. This crowd is filled with indignation.

The "Turn Loose and Pour It on Jesus" Crowd.

These are those who believe it should be poured on Jesus. "[They] sat at the table with Him." John 12:2.

★ ★ ★ ★ ★

The crowd that gets it done is the crowd that breaks the alabaster box, the crowd that turns loose of it all and pours it on the LORD Jesus.

One of those sitting at the table was Simon the leper. He'd been cleansed; he was at home with his family; he was enjoying the sweet fellowship of family and friends and especially the LORD Jesus. If it were not for the LORD Jesus, he would be in a place for lepers, separated for the rest of his life. If he were to comment, he would say, "Break it! Break it! Pour it all on Jesus!"

Lazarus, who had been dead, also sat with Jesus. If it were not for the LORD Jesus, he would be lying in some cold grave. If he had spoken up, he would have said, "Mary, give it all to Jesus!"

Those who have been touched by God, those who have been brought back to life, those who have been "quickened, who were dead in trespasses and sins" Ephesians 2:1. They are part of this crowd. They say, "Pour it all on Jesus!"

If there was ever a time in your life when you needed the blood of Jesus to cleanse your heart and every child of God needs that - then you ought to be a part of this crowd.

Every Christian is a part of one of these three crowds: the Judas crowd, the indignant crowd, or the break-the-alabaster-box crowd.

★ ★ ★ ★ ★

There is nothing that should be held back from Jesus. We need to pour it all out on the LORD. Through all of this - Mary's action and the reactions of Judas and the disciples - Jesus had been silent. He was just sitting there. Remember, He had been trying to prepare His disciples for what lay ahead.

He had tried to tell them about Calvary and His death before, but Simon Peter rebuked Him. When He tried to tell them again, James and John, by way of their mother, tried to get the best seats in the kingdom.

He must have been wondering how to get their attention on what He wanted to tell them.

THE LORD'S RESPONSE TO MARY'S GIFT

What was the LORD Jesus' reaction? There is an interesting statement in Matthew 26:10 that makes you stop and meditate: "When Jesus understood it...."

He was sitting there as the crowds reacted to Mary's action. Judas made his first comment recorded in the Bible, and the disciples let their opinion be known. Simon the leper and Lazarus who had been dead were sitting at the table with Jesus, watching Him as they smelled this ointment and saw Mary wipe His feet with her hair.

Throughout all of this, the LORD Jesus was silent. And then the Word of God says, "When Jesus understood it...."

★ ★ ★ ★ ★

In other words, God revealed it to Him, and He understood it. He understood that God had found someone who had such a love for the LORD Jesus and wanted so much to do something for God that God put this inside her heart. Look at what Jesus did when 'He understood it.'

He Accepted It

The LORD Jesus accepted it. "And Jesus said, Let her alone; why trouble ye her? she hath wrought a good work on Me." Mark 14:6.

The goal of Christians ought to be to please God, to be acceptable to Him, pleasing Him with our lives, doing what He wants us to do.

"Let the words of my mouth, and the meditation of my heart, be <u>acceptable in Thy sight</u>, O Lord, my strength, and my redeemer." Psalms. 19:14.

"I beseech you therefore, brethren, by the mercies of God, that ye present your bodies a living sacrifice, holy, <u>acceptable unto God</u>, which is your reasonable service.

And be not conformed to this world: but be ye transformed by the renewing of your mind, that ye may prove what is that good, and <u>acceptable</u>, and perfect, will of God." Romans 12:1, 2.

Are we living a life that is acceptable to the LORD? The highest goal of Christian living is to please the LORD. The LORD Jesus, who is our example said, "I do always those

★ ★ ★ ★ ★

things that please Him." John 8:29.

He Appraised It

The LORD Jesus appraised it. "She hath done what she could: she is come aforehand to anoint My body to the burying." Mark 14:8.

It was worth something, and He put this price tag on it. Mary had done it all. There was nothing else she could have done.

Don't you want to meet the LORD someday and hear Him say, "You have done what you could"? Each one of us is given different abilities, different talents and different things we can do.

We have different measures of faith, but it is wonderful to come across a child of God who takes what God has given them and puts it all on the altar. One day that person will hear the LORD Jesus say, "You have done what you could."

I want to take advantage of the opportunities that God has given me; I want to do with my life all that can be accomplished in my life. That's the way Mary felt. She wanted to do something for God with her life, and the LORD Jesus said, "Let her alone; why trouble ye her? she hath wrought a good work on Me."

"She hath done what she could: she is come aforehand to anoint My body to the burying." Mark 14:6,8.

★ ★ ★ ★ ★

After accepting it and appraising it, Jesus did something else.

He Anointed It

The LORD Jesus anointed it and used it. "Verily I say unto you, Wheresoever this gospel shall be preached in the whole world, there shall also this, that this woman hath done, be told for a memorial of her." Matthew 26:13.

I've always been amazed at what God revealed to women in the Bible and how He used them in a mighty way - here is one of them! While Judas was whining about the loss of income from Mary's act; while the disciples were wondering how things were going to work out for them, Mary was waiting on God.

Mary saw what others could not see. As she looked at the LORD Jesus sitting at the table with Lazarus and Simon, she saw what Christ came to do.

On one side are those who are dead in trespasses and sin. On the other are those who are unclean because of sin. God put in her heart to break the box and pour the ointment because it is a picture of what was going to happen on Calvary.

The LORD Jesus was going to shed His blood on Calvary. Calvary is not a waste. Calvary is not God's measuring a little. Calvary is where Christ was broken and poured out for those who are dead in trespasses and sins, and for those who are unclean because of sin.

★ ★ ★ ★ ★

God put this in Mary's heart and the LORD Jesus understood that this object lesson could be used to help others understand what Calvary is all about.

As soon as the LORD put it in her heart, she ran and grabbed up her alabaster box, went back to the table, walked past Judas and the disciples, broke her alabaster box and poured out all its contents over Jesus.

Then she knelt down on her hands and knees and wiped His feet with her hair.

God has the power to give life to those who are dead in trespasses, and the blood of Jesus cleanses us from sin. No one is so far gone that God cannot save him, or so far away from Him that He can't cleanse his heart.

Mary didn't pour the ointment from the box; she broke the box and poured all of it on Him, and the Bible says that "Jesus understood it." He realized that Mary saw Calvary and that she understood that Calvary was not a waste; it would be the place of salvation, the place of cleansing.

She saw that enough blood would be shed on Calvary to reach the world and that the cleansing blood of Jesus would wash away our sin. Nobody else saw that, not even His disciples; and when Jesus understood that, He anointed it and taught a great lesson.

"When Jesus understood it, He said unto them, Why trouble ye the woman? for she hath wrought a good work upon Me.

★ ★ ★ ★ ★

For ye have the poor always with you; but Me ye have not always.

For in that she hath poured this ointment on My body, she did it for My burial.

Verily I say unto you, Wheresoever this gospel shall be preached in the whole world, there shall also this, that this woman hath done, be told for a memorial of her." Matthew 26:10-13.

This helps us to understand the Gospel. The LORD Jesus was able to anoint this act and use it in such a mighty way that for nearly two thousand years this act of love and kindness and dedication has been used to stir the hearts of people to come to Jesus.

It has been used to stir the hearts of God's people to break their alabaster boxes at the feet of Jesus and pour it all on the LORD.

MARY'S REWARD

What was Mary's reward? The LORD said, "Tell it! Tell this story!" That's what I'm doing now because He wants us to see Mary's reward. I don't know what it will be like, but I know this: it is going to be exciting!

★ ★ ★ ★ ★

Can you imagine that one of these days - and I believe it is soon - the LORD is coming? This generation of Christians is closer to the LORD's second coming than any other generation that has ever lived! That ought to excite you!

"For the Lord Himself shall descend from heaven with a shout, with the voice of the archangel, and with the trump of God: and the dead in Christ shall rise first:

Then we which are alive and remain shall be caught up together with them in the clouds, to meet the Lord in the air: and so shall we ever be with the Lord.

Wherefore comfort one another with these words." I Thessalonians 4:16-18.

That "shout" is going to change the world! We're going to get a glorified body and have the mind of Christ. The last person saved is the first one to appear at the Judgment Seat of Christ, and then we will go all the way back to the first ones saved.

We're going to see all those who made it possible for us to read this message. I'm going to meet the man who went by a nursing home facility and led my father to the LORD, and we had no idea that he had been saved.

We're going to see that man, and we'll see the ones who led him to Christ, and those that led them to Christ, and we'll work our way back to the disciples.

★ ★ ★ ★ ★

What a time that's going to be! No wonder the apostle Paul said, "Holding forth the word of life; that I may rejoice in the day of Christ, that I have not run in vain, neither laboured in vain" Philippians 2:16.

Imagine the celebration that we're going to have with a glorified body, and the mind of Christ, and the ability to understand all that took place down through the centuries in order for us to know Jesus! What a day of rejoicing that will be! Then we're going to meet Mary. I don't know what she did with her life.

As far as I know, she did not become a missionary, but 'she did all that she could' - she broke her alabaster box.

Then the LORD Jesus did something so kind and gracious: He challenged everybody who ever preaches the Gospel to tell the story. He loved her so much, and what she did was so powerful that He wanted every man who ever preached to 'tell this story as a memorial to her.' What she did that day is not finished. Her act of kindness and dedication is still making an investment to this day.

Every time this story is mentioned, a reward is being stored up for her, and one of these days she'll receive her reward, and we'll see it. I cannot wait to see what God pours on this woman as a result of her one act of love for her Savior.

★ ★ ★ ★ ★

WILL YOU BREAK YOUR ALABASTER BOX?

This story reminds us that it is so important to do what God puts in our hearts to do. What we do has an effect and an influence on every generation to follow.

Somewhere a handful of people with an alabaster box made your church a reality. Every time that God has ever done anything, somebody has had to break an alabaster box. Can you imagine what would get done in this world if everyone who is saved would, with a grateful heart, bring his or her alabaster box and break it for the LORD?

The truth of the matter is, many are just like Judas and the disciples who were sitting there at the table that day with Jesus. Simon the leper and Lazarus, who had been raised from the dead, were clueless. But Mary saw it.

What do you see? Do you see the work of God? Do you see that your church is not just a place to meet but that it is a work of God? The LORD puts in the hearts of His people what He wants done. What has God put in your heart to do?

Years ago, we had a missionary give his testimony in our church. As a ten-year-old boy, he had surrendered at a camp to become a missionary. When he was thirty years old, he was on the mission field in a village, and he met a man who had gotten saved twenty years prior to their meeting.

The man said, "The missionary that led me to the LORD knelt down beside me and my family and prayed that God

★ ★ ★ ★ ★

would touch somebody's heart and that he would come to this village and be a missionary." Twenty years later he saw the answer to that prayer. God heard those people praying, and He reached over and touched a ten-year-old child's heart and he surrendered to become a missionary. That is the way the LORD works.

What is God doing in your life? Has He spoken to you about something? Has He put a desire in your heart to do something? Maybe there is something special you can do for God's work. Will you break your alabaster box and pour it on the LORD Jesus? You'll be glad you did. Remember;

★ ★ ★ ★ ★

People Are Just People

By Tom Sexton

People are just people, no matter the color of their skin.

At our best we are just people, flawed women and men.

Naked we're born with so much to learn,

At the end of our journey, naked we'll return.

Some make it big and others stay the same.

Some have great talent and achieve worldwide fame.

Some give their life to make all that they can.

Some come to Christ and faithfully follow His plan.

Some make fortunes and have the world in their hands.

Some lift up Jesus the Saviour for every man.

Millions who were in darkness have been given new birth,

By the ones taking the Gospel to the ends of the earth.

Yes, people are just people no matter when they live,

But the ones who count, are the ones who give.

★ ★ ★ ★ ★

★ ★ ★ ★ ★

PULLING DOWN YOUR BARNS

The Sin Of Covetousness

The Lord Jesus takes advantage of a brother's greed to warn His followers of the dangers of covetousness.

The man the Lord Jesus is telling us about is a man who would agree with the thinking of believers in our day. He made a decision to keep the overflow of the blessing of God on his life.

I recently heard a Christian leader say to a group of followers of Christ how much money they will need to live comfortably after they retire. He said, "In our world today retirees need 1.5 million dollars to make sure they do not run out of money before they die.

His speech convinced many to hold on to more of their overflow and invest it in their future. The man Jesus introduces us to in this story is a first-century man, with twenty-first century thinking.

Jesus said, "Take heed, and beware of covetousness: for a man's life consisteth not in the abundance of the things which he possesseth.

★ ★ ★ ★ ★

And he spake a parable unto them, saying, The ground of a certain rich man brought forth plentifully: And he thought within himself, saying, What shall I do, because I have no room where to bestow my fruits?

And he said, This will I do: I will pull down my barns, and build greater; and there will I bestow all my fruits and my goods. And I will say to my soul, Soul, thou hast much goods laid up for many years; take thine ease, eat, drink, and be merry.

But God said unto him, *Thou* fool, this night thy soul shall be required of thee: then whose shall those things be, which thou hast provided? So is he that layeth up treasure for himself, and is not rich toward God." Luke 12:13-21.

God has much to say concerning the sin of covetousness. The Bible says, "Thou shalt not covet" and, "he that hateth covetousness shall prolong his days." Exodus 20:17 & Proverbs 28:16.

This parable has a great truth for us to learn; a powerful lesson in these days. As we look into this parable, it does not seem to be a bad thing for this man, with barns too small for his goods, to build a bigger barn. However, not everything is what it appears to be on the surface.

I would like to take the word "BARNS" and do an acrostic using the words: **B**arn, **A**bility, **R**esponsibility, **N**eed and **S**in, to teach the great truth of this parable.

- The **Barns** we build. "…my barns…" v. 18.

★ ★ ★ ★ ★

Barns have a purpose. This man said he needed a place to "…
bestow all my fruits and my goods." The Bible says, "If any
provide not for his own, and specially for those of his own
house, he hath denied the faith, and is worse than an infidel."
I Timothy 5:8.

Barns were needed to store for the future. Some people have
a need for one barn. Some have a need for many barns. This
man did not get in trouble with the Lord for building barns.
The Lord does not tell us how big nor how many barns we
should build.

Barns represent what we need for our families. Do you need
a little car, or do you need a big car? Do you need a one-bed-
room home, or do you need five bedrooms for your family?

Jesus did not say "I will build your barn." Jesus expects men
to know what kind of barn to build and what size of barn to
build for their families. Barns represent everything we need
for the care of our families. Make sure you have a barn that
works for you.

What does your family need to stay on the path God has for
them? Build it!

- The **Ability** of God to fill our barns.

The Bible says, "Honour the LORD with thy substance, and
with the first fruits of all thine increase: So, shall thy <u>barns</u>
be filled with plenty, and thy presses shall burst out with new

★ ★ ★ ★ ★

wine." Proverbs 3:9-10. God can fill our barns no matter how big they are if we honor Him with our first fruits.

God says, "…I will…open the windows of heaven, and pour you out a blessing, that there shall not be room enough to receive it." Malachi 3:10. God will overflow our barns if we <u>bring</u> the tithe to the storehouse (the church).

The Lord Jesus said, "Give, and it shall be given unto you; good measure, pressed down, and shaken together, and running over, shall men give into your bosom." Luke 6:38. If we give to the cause of Christ and the Gospel, Jesus will speak to the hearts of people to bless us.

Paul reminded the church in Philippi that God would supply all their needs for reaching the world with the Gospel. He said, "But my God shall supply all your need according to His riches in glory by Christ Jesus." Philippians 4:19.

The Lord can do more than just fill our barns. He will overflow our barns with blessings. You build the barn, honor the Lord, invest in the Gospel, and He will fill your barns.

- The **Responsibility** we have as a child of God.

The Bible teaches us, "For unto whomsoever much is given, of him shall be much required…" Luke 12:48.

We are to, "Charge them that are rich in this world, that they be not highminded, nor trust in uncertain riches, but in the living God, who giveth us richly all things to enjoy;

★ ★ ★ ★ ★

That they do good, that they be rich in good works, ready to distribute, willing to communicate; Laying up in store for themselves a good foundation against the time to come, that they may lay hold on eternal life." I Timothy 6:17-19.

Paul said, "I am debtor…"to all who are without Christ in the world. (Romans 1:14). We are responsible to God to get the Gospel to the lost. "For none of us liveth to himself, and no man dieth to himself." Romans 14:7.

- The **Need** that he failed to meet.

"But God said unto him, Thou fool, this night thy soul shall be required of thee: then who's shall those things be, which thou hast provided?" v 20.

God did not bless this man just so he could build a bigger barn and keep all the blessings of the Lord for himself. There was a need that he could have used the blessings, the over-flow of God, to meet. There is a need that the Lord wants us to meet using our overflow of blessings.

- The **Sin** that captured his heart.

Jesus said, "…Take heed, and beware of covetousness: for a man's life consisteth not in the abundance of the things which he possesseth." v. 15. The reason God called him a fool was because he failed to do, with the increase, what God wanted done. God does not bless us just so we can build more or bigger barns.

★ ★ ★ ★ ★

The sin of covetousness, as illustrated in this parable, is keeping the increase or the overflow.

Once we have chosen the barn we need, it is time to stop pulling down our barns or building bigger ones. The Bible says, "But godliness with contentment is great gain." I Timothy 6:6. When will we say enough is enough?

"He that loveth silver shall not be satisfied with silver; nor he that loveth abundance with increase: this is also vanity. When goods increase, they are increased that eat them: and what good is there to the owners thereof, saving the beholding of them with their eyes…There is a sore evil which I have seen under the sun, namely, riches kept for the owners thereof to their hurt." Ecclesiastes 5:10-11,13.

Let me illustrate this great truth.

The Lord Jesus said that when he comes again that it will be as it was in the days of Lot. Jesus said, "And as it was in the …days of Lot…Even thus shall it be in the day when the Son of man is revealed." Luke 17:27-30.

It is true that the world is becoming more and more like Sodom and Gomorrah, but the other side of the coin is that believers are also becoming more like Lot in their thinking. Lot was a believer who loved what he had more than he loved the One who blessed him with it.

★ ★ ★ ★ ★

Every decision Lot made, that led to his destruction, was made in order for him to keep everything God blessed him with. (Gensis 13:5-13).

Today we have many Lot-minded believers living in a Gomorrah-minded world. They want to keep everything for themselves. They are pulling down their barns in order to build bigger ones. Stop building more barns because, God will give through you much more than He will give to you, if you allow Him to do so.

★ ★ ★ ★ ★

★ ★ ★ ★ ★

★ ★ ★ ★ ★

STEWARDSHIP QUESTIONS

"Moreover it is required in stewards, that a man be found faithful" I Corinthians 4:2.

The questions that make up this list have been gleaned from many followers of Christ.

These questions cover all three areas of giving: the tithe, our offerings, and faith promise-giving. Many questions did not make the list, questions that no serious-minded child of God would ask, such as, "May I deduct my gas expense for going to church from my tithe?" or my favorite, "Can I deduct the cost of my wife's new Easter dress from my tithe?"

May the LORD Jesus help us better understand this very important subject of stewardship, knowing that one day we will all give an account to Him.

"For we must all appear before the judgment seat of Christ; that every one may receive the things done in his body, according to that he hath done, whether it be good or bad" II Corinthians 5:10.

★ ★ ★ ★ ★

1. What is stewardship?

2. What does the LORD own?

3. What is the tithe?

4. Is tithing a practice for this age?

5. Should I tithe if I cannot afford to?

6. Should I bring my tithe to the local church?

7. What is the difference between giving and tithing?

8. What is faith promise giving?

9. Is money evil?

10. Should a Christian seek earthly possessions?

11. Does God want Christians to prosper in this world?

12. If I give, will I have financial problems?

13. Why do unsaved people prosper?

14. May I use the tithe if I need it?

15. Was Jesus a tither?

16. Should people in full-time Christian work tithe?

★ ★ ★ ★ ★

17. Does the church need money (my money)?

18. Can I choose what my tithe goes to?

19. Should poor people be asked to give?

20. Should someone tithe who is in debt?

21. Should I tithe on my gross income or my take-home pay?

22. How much offering should I give above the tithe?

23. Should young children be taught to tithe and give?

24. What if my husband or wife is lost—should I still tithe?

25. Should I send my gift to the missionary through the church?

26. Should I tithe on a gift or inheritance?

27. Should I tithe on my income tax refund check or my bonus?

28. Can I deduct a mission's trip, Christian school, or camp from the tithe?

29. Should I give to a brother in need?

30. Why should I give to the poor?

★ ★ ★ ★ ★

1. What is stewardship?

"Let a man so account of us, as of the ministers of Christ, and stewards of the mysteries of God. Moreover it is required in stewards, that a man be found faithful" I Corinthians 4:1-2.

Also read Luke 12:42; Titus 1:7; and I Peter 4:10.

To be a steward means to manage someone's household or estate. A steward is not the one who owns but the one who controls and makes decisions concerning another's affairs and wealth.

As "…stewards of the manifold grace of God" I Peter 4:10, we will one day give an account to God, II Corinthians 5:10.

2. What does the LORD own?

"For every beast of the forest is Mine, and the cattle upon a thousand hills" Psalm 50:10.

"The silver is Mine, and the gold is Mine, saith the LORD of hosts" Haggai 2:8.

"The earth is the LORD'S, and the fulness thereof; the world, and they that dwell therein" Psalm 24:1.

"What? know ye not that your body is the temple of the Holy Ghost which is in you, which ye have of God, and ye are not your own? For ye are bought with a price: there-

★ ★ ★ ★ ★

fore glorify God in your body, and in your spirit, which are God's" I Corinthians 6:19-20.

These verses teach that the LORD owns 100% of everything, not just 10%. If we understand that we belong to the LORD, we realize that nothing is ours. We are only stewards. "Moreover it is required in stewards, that a man be found faithful" I Corinthians 4:2.

3. What is the tithe?

"Will a man rob God? Yet ye have robbed Me. But ye say, Wherein have we robbed Thee? In tithes and offerings. Ye are cursed with a curse: for ye have robbed Me, even this whole nation. <u>Bring</u> ye all the tithes <u>into</u> the storehouse, that there may be meat in Mine house…" Malachi 3:8-10.

A tithe is 10%. "…The tenth shall be holy unto the LORD" Leviticus 27:32. It is holy because it belongs to the LORD.

When we tithe the LORD does three things for us according to Malachi 3:8-11. He prospers us by opening the windows of Heaven. He promises to rebuke the devourer (the devil). He protects the fruit of our lives.

We are to <u>bring</u> the tithe <u>into</u> the storehouse on "…the first day of the week…" I Corinthians 16:1-2. Sunday is the first day of the week, and the church is the storehouse.

★ ★ ★ ★ ★

4. Is tithing a practice for this age?

Yes, tithing has been God's plan for the ages, from the Garden of Eden unto the day in which we live. Tithing was practiced before the Law. Abraham gave a tithe to Melchizedek (who was a type of Christ) in Genesis 14:20: "…he gave him tithes of all."

Tithing was taught and practiced under the Law. "…All the tithe…is the LORD'S…" Leviticus 27:30. Tithing was confirmed by the LORD Jesus. "…Ye pay tithe…these ought ye to have done, and not to leave the other undone" Matthew 23:23. Tithing is taught and practiced all through the Bible and is not limited to one age.

Tithing is for this age

5. Should I tithe if I cannot afford to?

As we have seen, 100% belongs to the LORD. He gives us 90% and only keeps 10%. We don't give Him a tithe as much as He gives us 90%. Before He gave it to us, He owned 100%. Now He claims 10%. This is what He is talking about in Malachi 3:8 when He asks, "Will a man rob God?" The tithe is not ours to keep; it belongs to the LORD.

The child of God should not be considering the question of whether or not they can afford to tithe, but can they afford not to tithe. They should ask themselves if they want to live the life of a thief. A good steward does not keep more than

★ ★ ★ ★ ★

his partner says. We are God's partners according to I Corinthians 3:9: "For we are labourers together with God…"

6. Should I bring my tithe to the local church?

"<u>Bring</u> ye all the tithes <u>into</u> the storehouse…" Malachi 3:10. The church is the New Testament storehouse according to I Corinthians 16:1-2: "…as I have given order to the churches… Upon the first day of the week let every one of you lay by him in store, as God hath prospered him…"

The church is God's storehouse in the New Testament, and every Christian should <u>bring</u> their tithe to their local church. God's Word says in Malachi 3 that we should "<u>bring</u>" the tithe, not give it. It is not ours to give. It belongs to the LORD (Leviticus 27:30-32).

7. What is the difference between giving and tithing?

"Give, and it shall be given unto you; good measure, pressed down, and shaken together, and running over, shall men give into your bosom. For with the same measure that ye mete withal it shall be measured to you again" Luke 6:38.

Many people think that the tithe is giving. But the tithe belongs to the LORD. Tithing is not giving; it is bringing. Our giving is out of the 90% we have left after the tithe. This is the area from which we receive the blessing of the LORD.

The reward of giving is a God-blessed life here and now, and treasures in Heaven. "But lay up for yourselves treasures

★ ★ ★ ★ ★

in heaven, where neither moth nor rust doth corrupt, and where thieves do not break through nor steal" Matthew 6:20.

Because of our people's willingness to give above their tithe and to give an offering to the work of the LORD, we are able to do more in missions, Sunday School, the bus ministry, and special projects of our church.

8. What is faith promise giving?

"…Beyond their power they were willing…" II Corinthians 8:1-5.

Other Bible verses to consider are: Philippians 4:10-19; II Corinthians 9:6-8; and Romans 12:8.

Faith promise-giving is asking the LORD to let us give beyond ourselves. It is for Christians who have become faithful tithers and have given sacrificially out of their budget for the cause of Christ, yet want to do more, "beyond their power."

The tithe belongs to God—we bring it. Giving is out of the 90% we have, and when we give, we get in on God's great work. It is our investment (Matthew 6:19-21).

Faith promise-giving is asking God to lay upon our hearts an amount that He will give through us. Often this gift will come to us beyond our normal income. When God gives that amount to us by some way we did not expect, our faith and confidence in the LORD is increased, and we are able to give "beyond" ourselves.

★ ★ ★ ★ ★

Faith promise-giving is allowing God to give through us. It is not how God raises money, but how He matures His children. Our faith is increased when we see the LORD give through us. The LORD will give through us what we are not able to give without Him.

9. Is money evil?

"For the love of money is the root of all evil: which while some coveted after, they have erred from the faith, and pierced themselves through with many sorrows" I Timothy 6:10.

"Charge them that are rich in this world, that they be not highminded, nor trust in uncertain riches, but in the living God, who giveth us richly all things to enjoy" I Timothy 6:17. No, money is not evil, but the Bible does say that "the love of money is the root of all evil."

Money was made to spend. It is called currency. There is nothing wrong with having money as long as we do not love it and we continue to spend it for the LORD and His work. Sadly, many Christians have "coveted after" it and destroyed their lives and their families. Very few people can handle wealth.

10. Should a Christian seek earthly possessions?

"And having food and raiment let us be therewith content" I Timothy 6:8.

★ ★ ★ ★ ★

"Let your conversation be without covetousness; and be content with such things as ye have: for He hath said, I will never leave thee, nor forsake thee" Hebrews 13:5.

The world says, "Get all you can and keep all you get." But Christians understand that this world will one day pass away (I John 2:15-17), and we cannot take it with us.

The LORD gives us "…all things to enjoy" I Timothy 6:17, and He wants us to enjoy our journey here on earth. We must remember that contentment only comes to those who live for the LORD (I Timothy 6:6). All that this world has to offer will not bring contentment.

Thank God for what He has given you, but remember, He is your joy and contentment.

11. Does God want Christians to prosper in this world?

"And Jesus answered and said, Verily I say unto you, There is no man that hath left house, or brethren, or sisters, or father, or mother, or wife, or children, or lands, for My sake, and the gospel's, But he shall receive an hundredfold now in this time, houses, and brethren, and sisters, and mothers, and children, and lands, with persecutions; and in the world to come eternal life" Mark 10:29-30.

"Beloved, I wish above all things that thou mayest prosper and be in health, even as thy soul prospereth" III John 2.

★ ★ ★ ★ ★

"The blessing of the LORD, it maketh rich, and He addeth no sorrow with it" Proverbs 10:22.

Also read Psalm 37:3; Proverbs 22:29; 3:9-10; and Malachi 3:10. There are many more portions of Scripture where the LORD promises to bless His children and to make their life prosperous.

He said to Joshua that if he would spend time in His Word and do what He said "…then thou shalt make thy way prosperous, and then thou shalt have good success" Joshua 1:8c.

Yes, God does want His children to prosper, but first they must learn to live right.

12. If I give, will I have financial problems?

"But my God shall supply all your need according to His riches in glory by Christ Jesus" Philippians 4:19.

Becoming faithful in giving will not change what we have sown. If we have made bad investments or over-extended ourselves, there will be a time of reaping (Galatians 6:7). God has promised to meet our needs, not our greeds. Faithfulness in giving will bring the blessing of God on our lives, and we can pray for a small crop in the fields we have sown foolishly.

The Word of God does say that Christ came to deliver (Psalm 107:20).

★ ★ ★ ★ ★

13. Why do unsaved people prosper?

"For I was envious at the foolish, when I saw the prosperity of the wicked" Psalm 73:3.

"Behold, these are the ungodly, who prosper in the world; they increase in riches. Until I went into the sanctuary of God; then understood I their end" Psalm 73:12,17.

"Fret not thyself because of evildoers, neither be thou envious against the workers of iniquity. For they shall soon be cut down like the grass, and wither as the green herb" Psalm 37:1-2.

Our vision is limited. We only see a small part of the big picture. This world will one day pass away (I John 2:15-17). What unsaved people invest their lives in will one day burn. Their prosperity is only one-sided. The child of God prospers in the things that money cannot buy.

The LORD Jesus said that the man who gained the whole world would give it all to have what God's children possess, eternal life (Matthew 16:26).

14. May I use the tithe if I need it?

"And all the tithe of the land, whether of the seed of the land, or of the fruit of the tree, is the LORD'S: it is holy unto the LORD. And if a man will at all redeem ought of his tithes, he shall add thereto the fifth part thereof" Leviticus 27:30-31.

★ ★ ★ ★ ★

This verse teaches us that if the tithe is kept, there should be added to it 20%. This sounds like God is being cruel to those who get into financial problems, but the truth is that He does not want His children to be under the curse (Malachi 3:8-10) which is on those who rob Him.

He does this to discourage any from violating His Word.

15. Was Jesus a tither?

"Which of you convinceth Me of sin?" John 8:46a.

The LORD Jesus asked a question that no one else could ask. He was willing to let all who knew Him try to find fault with Him.

He was known as the carpenter's son, and He was a carpenter before He began His public ministry. As a carpenter, He would have received wages and been expected to give.

If He was not a tither, someone would have said, "He's a God-robber." He was a tither, and we know how He felt about the Temple. If He failed to bring His tithe to the house of the LORD, this is when someone (the priest or rabbi) would have accused Him of violating the Scriptures.

16. Should people in full-time Christian work tithe?

"For this cause pay ye tribute also: for they are God's ministers, attending continually upon this very thing" Romans 13:6. "Moreover it is required in stewards, that a man be found faithful" I Corinthians 4:2.

★ ★ ★ ★ ★

Those in full-time work should be the ones leading the way in the area of giving. If a person in leadership is not a faithful steward, they are disqualified.

17. Does the church need money (my money)?

"Having land, sold it, and brought the money, and laid it at the apostles' feet" Acts 4:37.

A New Testament church is supported by its membership. If they are going to reach the world (Acts 1:8), they will need every member to give. Someone has said, "You can't reach the world and build a great church on spare time and pocket change." We should not ask, "Does the church need my money?" We should ask, "How can I give more through our church?"

18. Can I choose what my tithe goes to?

"And laid them down at the apostles' feet: and distribution was made unto every man according as he had need" Acts 4:35.

The tithe is to be brought and used where it is needed. We cannot designate the tithe, but we can give an offering to some ministry that is on our heart. If it is something that the local church is interested in doing or wants to have a part in, then members can give to it.

★ ★ ★ ★ ★

19. Should poor people be asked to give?

"And He looked up, and saw the rich men casting their gifts into the treasury. And He saw also a certain poor widow casting in thither two mites. And He said, Of a truth I say unto you, that this poor widow hath cast in more than they all" Luke 21:1-3.

All of God's people whether rich or poor are to be faithful stewards. People who give will have the blessing of God on their life. I have seen people in other parts of the world, who are truly poor people, give out of what they have. Some give chickens, eggs, produce from the garden, etc. All who give are blessed of God.

Poor people should be in on the blessings too.

20. Should someone tithe who is in debt?

"Will a man rob God? Yet ye have robbed Me. But ye say, Wherein have we robbed Thee? In tithes and offerings" Malachi 3:8.

People end up in debt for many reasons. Debt is a hard taskmaster, and it makes life difficult, but debt does not free the child of God from obeying Scripture. No thinking person would want to add, the curse in Malachi 3:8-10, to the heartache that is already caused by debt.

★ ★ ★ ★ ★

21. Should I tithe on my gross income or my take-home pay?

"Honour the LORD with thy substance, and with the first-fruits of all thine increase" Proverbs 3:9. Our income is our gross income; it is the firstfruits. Take-home pay may vary depending on deductions and other withholdings. A faithful Christian tithes on their gross income.

22. How much offering should I give above the tithe?

"Upon the first day of the week let every one of you lay by him in store, as God hath prospered him, that there be no gatherings when I come" I Corinthians 16:2.

What we give above the tithe or after the tithe is totally up to us. It is our investment in the LORD's work. It will result in treasures in Heaven (Matthew 6:19-21).

23. Should young children be taught to tithe and give?

"Teaching them to observe all things whatsoever I have commanded you: and, lo, I am with you alway, even unto the end of the world. Amen" Matthew 28:20.

Children should be taught to be good stewards. They should give their time, talents, and treasures to the LORD. It is never too early to teach stewardship. Giving to the LORD's work is a safeguard against "the love of money" I Timothy 6:10.

★ ★ ★ ★ ★

24. What if my husband or wife is lost—should I still tithe?

"Moreover it is required in stewards, that a man be found faithful" I Corinthians 4:2. "So then every one of us shall give account of himself to God" Romans 14:12.

"Obey them that have the rule over you, and submit your-selves: for they watch for your souls, as they that must give account, that they may do it with joy, and not with grief: for that is unprofitable for you" Hebrews 13:17.

The husband is the head of the home (Ephesians 5:23) and should lead the way regardless if his wife is saved or not. If the husband is lost and the wife is saved, she should certain-ly tithe on her income and let her husband know that, in order for her to be a faithful Christian (which will help her to be faithful to him), she must honor the LORD.

25. Should I send my gift to the missionary through the church?

"Neither was there any among them that lacked: for as many as were possessors of lands or houses sold them, and brought the prices of the things that were sold, And laid them down at the apostles' feet: and distribution was made unto every man according as he had need" Acts 4:34-35.

All giving, and especially to missionaries, should go through the local church. The church is commissioned to evangelize the world, and the church sends missionaries (Acts 13:1-5).

★ ★ ★ ★ ★

26. Should I tithe on a gift or inheritance?

"Every good gift and every perfect gift is from above, and cometh down from the Father of lights, with whom is no variableness, neither shadow of turning" James 1:17.

Yes, we are to be good stewards with all that comes into our lives. If we are faithful, the LORD will bring much more into our hands to be used for His work.

27. Should I tithe on my income tax refund check or my bonus?

"Every good gift and every perfect gift is from above, and cometh down from the Father of lights, with whom is no variableness, neither shadow of turning" James 1:17. "Honour the LORD with thy substance, and with the firstfruits of <u>all</u> thine increase" Proverbs 3:9.

If we have tithed on our gross income, we have already tithed on our income tax refund check. If we receive something that we did not earn or something that has not been tithed on, we should tithe on that part.

28. Can I deduct a mission's trip, Christian school, or camp from the tithe?

"And all the tithe of the land, whether of the seed of the land, or of the fruit of the tree, is the LORD'S: it is holy unto the LORD" Leviticus 27:30.

★ ★ ★ ★ ★

There are many expenses that occur in the raising of our children. We have the 90% that is ours after the tithe to take care of these.

29. Should I give to a brother in need?

"But whoso hath this world's good, and seeth his brother have need, and shutteth up his bowels of compassion from him, how dwelleth the love of God in him?" I John 3:17.

"And laid them down at the apostles' feet: and distribution was made unto every man according as he had need" Acts 4:35. Helping a hurting brother or sister in the LORD is something dear to the heart of our Saviour.

However, all giving should be done through the local church, because a brother's need may be something the LORD is using to get His wayward child back to the place of blessing. And we do not want people indebted to us; we want people to love the church.

30. Why should I give to the poor?

"Only they would that we should remember the poor; the same which I also was forward to do" Galatians 2:10.

Here are some promises to those who give to the poor.

► We shall be blessed.

★ ★ ★ ★ ★

"Then said He also to him that bade Him, When thou makest a dinner or a supper, call not thy friends, nor thy brethren, neither thy kinsmen, nor thy rich neighbors; lest they also bid thee again, and a recompence be made thee.

But when thou makest a feast, call the poor, the maimed, the lame, the blind: <u>And thou shalt be blessed</u>; for they cannot recompense thee: for thou shalt be recompensed at the resurrection of the just" Luke 14:12-14.

▶ **We shall have treasures in Heaven.**

"Jesus said unto him, If thou wilt be perfect, go and sell that thou hast, and give to the poor, and <u>thou shalt have treasure</u> in heaven: and come and follow Me." Matthew 19:21.

▶ **We shall be happy.**

"He that despiseth his neighbor sinneth: but he that hath mercy on the poor, <u>happy is he</u>." Proverbs 14:21.

▶ **God will repay us.**

"He that hath pity upon the poor lendeth unto the LORD; and that which he hath given will <u>He pay him again</u>." Proverbs 19:17.

▶ **God will hear our prayers.**

"Whoso stoppeth his ears at the cry of the poor, he also shall cry himself, but <u>shall not be heard</u>" Proverbs 21:13.

★ ★ ★ ★ ★

▶ **We shall not lack.**

"He that giveth unto the poor <u>shall not lack</u>: but he that hideth his eyes shall have many a curse" Proverbs 28:27.

▶ **The LORD will deliver us in time of trouble.**

"Blessed is he that considereth the poor: <u>the LORD will deliver him in time of trouble</u>. The LORD will preserve him, and keep him alive; and he shall be blessed upon the earth: and Thou wilt not deliver him unto the will of his enemies.

The LORD will strengthen him upon the bed of languishing: Thou wilt make all his bed in his sickness" Psalm 41:1

★ ★ ★ ★ ★

★ ★ ★ ★ ★

JESUS
THE WORLDS ONLY ETERNITY PLANNER

Jesus said, "Lay not up for yourselves treasures upon earth, where moth and rust doth corrupt, and where thieves break through and steal: But lay up for yourselves treasures in heaven, where neither moth nor rust doth corrupt, and where thieves do not break through nor steal:" Matthew 6:19-20.

We can hardly live a day without someone telling us how we can send what we have earned into our future. It seems everyone is caught up in building a life in their future. Now I know that is important.

Someone said, "You don't want to run out of money before you run out of life." Interesting. Then they say, "Are you set for life?" I get it. I want my wife to have enough cooking supplies for the holidays. We don't want to run out of cookies before we run out of the holidays.

There are many who can help you plan for retirement, but there is only ONE who has planned your forever, and that my friend, is JESUS.

★ ★ ★ ★ ★

Jesus truly is the world's only eternity planner. So, with this in mind, what do you want in your next life? This life is "a vapour that appeareth for a little time, and then vanisheth away." James 4:14. Our next life is forever. Good news, Jesus is our future life planner.

If people would listen to His advice, they would have a better forever. What advice does Jesus give concerning the forever life?

Make sure your name is on the official residence list of Heaven.

Jesus said, "rejoice, because your names are written in heaven." Luke 10:20. Make sure your name is written in Heaven. The Bible says, "And whosoever was not found written in the book of life was cast into the lake of fire." Revelation 20:15.

Our name is written in Heaven "in the Lamb's book of life" when we are born again.

If your name is written in Heaven, you will have a place to live. Jesus said, "In my Father's house are many mansions: if it were not so, I would have told you. I go to prepare a place for you." John 14:2. Your heavenly home comes fully furnished and it has a great view. You are going to love living there forever.

Tell your family and friends how they can join you in Heaven.

We read where "One of the two which heard John speak, and followed him, was Andrew, Simon Peter's brother. He first

★ ★ ★ ★ ★

findeth his own brother Simon, and saith unto him, We have found the Messias, which is, being interpreted, the Christ. And he brought him to Jesus." John 1:40-41

Six powerful words, "And he brought him to Jesus." Jesus encouraged Andrew to bring his brother to Him. Jesus wants families to be together in Heaven.

If we will bring our family and friends to Jesus, He will take care of the rest. Don't go to Heaven without telling the people you love how to know Christ as their personal Saviour.

Where do we begin? Begin by telling your family what the Lord has done for you, and tell your friends the same.

Send some treasures ahead of you to Heaven.

Jesus said, "Lay not up for yourselves treasures upon earth, where moth and rust doth corrupt, and where thieves break through and steal: But lay up for yourselves treasures in heaven, where neither moth nor rust doth corrupt, and where thieves do not break through nor steal:" Matthew 6:19-20.

Jesus said in Revelation 3:18, "buy of me gold." How much of Heavens "gold" is in your heavenly portfolio? The only "treasures" we take with us to Heaven is people. Do you know people who need to hear the Gospel? Invest in Heaven by investing in God's work. Your "treasures in heaven" will testify of your love for Jesus.

★ ★ ★ ★ ★

Be ready for your departure to Heaven.

Jesus said, "Be therefore also ready: for in such an hour as ye think not the Son of man cometh." Matthew 24:44. When He comes, our time is up, there may not be time to say good-bye. Our Heavenly treasure is "kept by the power of God." He protects it from "moth, rust" and "thieves." These are three things that have the power to destroy earthly treasures.

Our Heavenly treasure increases in value when the people we reach invest their lives in the Lord's work. Paul encouraged the people he reached with the Gospel by saying, "Holding forth the word of life: that I may rejoice in the day of Christ, that I have not run in vain, neither laboured in vain." Philippians 2:16.

In other words, keep investing what you have been given; keep investing the Gospel. It was the investing of their lives, in the Lord's work, that made it gain in value.

We grow to love our treasure in Heaven more as time goes on. We can truly say about the people that have influenced our lives, "I thank my God upon every remembrance of you," Philippians 1:3

What makes Heaven's treasure so valuable is people we love are there. Do you have anyone in Heaven you love?

Very few people think about "treasures in heaven." However, people do think about their retirement, which may never happen.

★ ★ ★ ★ ★

Talk to your future planner, Jesus, and ask Him today about some investments you can make with your life.

Jesus Wants You To Live Your Forever In Heaven.

Acknowledge you are a sinner. The Bible says, "As it is written, There is none righteous, no, not one…For all have sinned, and come short of the glory of God;" Romans 3:10,23.

Believe Christ died for you. The Bible says, "For the wages of sin is death; but the gift of God is eternal life through Jesus Christ our Lord." "God commendeth His love toward us, in that, while we were yet sinners, Christ died for us." Romans 6:23, 5:8.

Call upon Him to save you. The Bible says, "That if thou shalt confess with thy mouth the Lord Jesus, and shalt believe in thine heart that God hath raised him from the dead, thou shalt be saved." Romans 10:9.

If you would be willing to turn to God in repentance and faith, pray this prayer:

"LORD, I know that I am a sinner, and I believe You died and rose again for me. I trust You to forgive me and deliver me from my sin. Come into my heart and save me. Help me to live for You. In Jesus' name, Amen." Everlasting life is ours when we receive Christ as our personal Saviour. God bless you.

★ ★ ★ ★ ★

Forever With Jesus

By Tom Sexton

Knowing You LordMakes my life worth living

With all its twists and all its turns

The time we have shared together

Is what my heart forever yearns

Everyone lives somewhere forever

One day we'll see it's true

My forever would be so lonely

If Your love I never knew

Your love for me has never altered

No matter what I've gone through

And when this journey is over

I choose my forever to be lived with You

Yes, everyone lives somewhere forever

Your love for me will never die, 'tis true

That's why I'm choosing my forever

To be lived in Heaven with you

★ ★ ★ ★ ★

Quotes on Stewardship

Tithing is God trusting us with His great wealth.

Tithing is not giving and giving is not tithing. Tithing is bringing.

The hole you give through is the same hole God gives through to you—make it big.

You will reap more than you sow; God will return to you in multiplied form.

Tithing is an acknowledgement of ownership.

God loves a cheerful giver, but He will take it from a grouch.

Tithing is an adventure in blessing; it is an opportunity to "prove" God.

Tithing is a starting point for giving. It opens the door to greater giving.

Tithing adds love to our living, grace to our giving, and power to our praying.

★ ★ ★ ★ ★

Giving is the joy of partnership with Christ.

Give according to your income lest God make your income according to your giving.

God's bank remains open regardless of the circumstances.

We possess, but God owns. We are God's so all we have is God's.

If all we have is God's property, then Satan is a trespasser.

God will never be a debtor to any man; no one ever out-gives God.

Those slow to plant will be slow to harvest.

The more you put in, the more you get out.

Faith giving will increase your living.

Planting a bigger field means reaping a bigger harvest.

Money was made to spend; spend it for God.

I'm giving while I'm living so I'm knowing where it's going.

★ ★ ★ ★ ★

★ ★ ★ ★ ★

For more helpful information visit

www.FiveStarChristianMinistries.com